Italian Cookbook

1001 Days of Easy & Exquisite Mediterranean Recipes for Pasta and Pizza Lovers

(David Dolcevita)

Table of Contents

Introduction

It is my pleasure to have written

"Italian Cookbook" for your cooking needs. The book is written so it is simple to understand and prepared using ingredients available in most markets. The titles and some ingredients are still in the Italian format, so they are easily recognized.

According to my research the first Italian course is described as follows:

First course is considered a primo. It is comprised of hot cuisine and is often lighter than the second course but heavier than the antipasto. Any primo dish must include non-meat items, such as risotto, pasta with seafood or vegetarian sauces, broth and soup, lasagna, gnocchi with polenta or crespelle, and casseroles.

You will also be using extra-virgin olive oil for your dining needs since it is the "Italian Cookbook" way of living. You will also enjoy its veggie favorites, including artichokes, arugula, broccolini, celery, fennel, portobello mushrooms, radicchio, and lacinato kale. Each segment is designed for your reading pleasure and the improvement of your cooking skills using Italian cuisine as your palette. Let us get started on the delicious first course!

Prepare to become the Italian chef!
Dear Reader,

We would like to express our heartfelt gratitude for choosing
"Italian Cookbook"
as your culinary companion. As you embark on a delightful journey through the flavors of the Mediterranean, we invite you to savor each dish with passion and love.

Your satisfaction is our greatest reward, and we kindly request you to consider leaving an excellent review. Your feedback is invaluable, as it not only encourages us but also helps fellow food enthusiasts discover the joy of Mediterranean cuisine.

Bon appétit!

Chapter 1: Italian Soup & Broth Favorites

Alphabet Pastina with Vegetable Broth

Total Time: 25 min.
Yields Provided: 4 portions

Ingredients Used:

- Water (3 quarts)
- Alphabet Pastina (.75 lb.)
- Onion (.25 cup)
- Tomatoes (.5 cup)
- Carrot (.5 cup)
- Fresh parsley (2 tbsp.)
- Bay leaves (2)
- Olive oil (2 tbsp.)
- Optional: Grated Parmigiano

Instructions:

1. Finely chop the veggies.
2. Add water and all the fixings (omit the pastina) to a soup pot.
3. Once boiling, let it simmer (15 min.)
4. Add the pastina and simmer till it is al dente.
5. Serve with some grated Parmigiano, optionally.

Wine Favorites: Californian Chardonnay

Chicken Gnocchi Soup

Total Time: 25 min.
Yields Provided: 8 portions

Ingredients Used:

- Olive oil (1 tbsp.)
- Butter (3 tbsp.)
- Celery (.5 cup)
- Garlic cloves (2)
- Onion (1 cup)
- Plain flour (.25 cup)
- Half-&-Half (2 cups)
- Chicken broth (14 oz. can*)
- Fresh spinach leaves (1 cup)
- Fresh thyme (1 tbsp.)
- Carrots (1 cup)
- Chicken breast – cooked (1 cup)
- Potato gnocchi (16 oz. pkg.)
- Black pepper & salt (as desired)

Instructions:

1. First, dice/mince the chicken, onion, celery, and garlic. Shred the carrots and chop the spinach.
2. Prepare a stock pot or large pan using a medium heat setting to warm the oil and butter. Raise the heat setting to reach med-high to sauté the garlic, celery, and onion until softened.
3. Make a roux by mixing in the flour (1 min.). Mix in the half & half and broth, stirring till it thickens as desired. *Note: For a thinner soup, use two cans of broth.
4. Toss in the prepared chicken, spinach, carrots, gnocchi, and thyme to simmer until done (5 min.). Serve with a dusting of pepper and salt.

Wine Favorites:
- Californian Pinot Noir - red wine, dry, oaked.
- Burgundy Chardonnay
- Valpolicella Ripasso - red wine, dry, oaked. Corvina, Rondinella, Molinara, Negrara, Veneto.

Clam & Pumpkin Soup

Total Time: 50 min.
Yields Provided: 4 portions

Ingredients Used:

- Pumpkin (400 g)
- Black pepper & salt
- Potatoes (2 small)
- Leek (1)
- Onion (1 small)
- Rosemary sprig (1)
- Parsley (1 bunch)
- Preserved clams in brine (1 large jar) or Anchovy fillets
- Olive oil
- To Serve: Amica Chips Frumì croutons – crispy used
- Suggested: Hand-held blender

Instructions:

1. Peel the pumpkin and chop the onion. Slice the leek and dice the potatoes.
2. Lightly sauté the leek and onion in a lightly oiled skillet (2 teaspoons/as needed).
3. Next, toss in the prepared potatoes, pumpkin, rosemary, and salt as desired. Wait a few minutes for the flavors to meld.
4. Pour in hot water (1 liter), cover, and simmer (1/2 hr.).
5. Drain the clams, add the preserving fluid to the sauce, and simmer with no lid (5 min.).
6. Blend the sauce till it is velvety.
7. Season the clams with pepper, a portion of oil, and minced parsley.
8. Mix in about two-thirds of the clams to the sauce.
9. Serve the cream in bowls, garnishing with the remaining clams.

Wine Favorites: Test your palette with one of these favorites:
- Müller Thurgau Frizzante delle Venezie IGT
- Astraio Viognier Maremma Toscana DOC
- Soave DOC

Minestrone di Verdure

Total Time: 28-30 min.
Yields Provided: 4 portions

Ingredients Used:

The Minestrone:
- Mixed vegetables: Potato, cabbage, celery, carrot, aubergine & courgette (2.25 lb./1 kg)
- Garlic clove (1)
- Onion (1)
- Stock - beef - chicken or vegetable (4.25 pints)
- Tubettini pasta (5.33 oz./150 g)
- Borlotti beans (14 ⅛ oz./400 g)
- Parmesan - freshly grated (1.5 oz./40 g)
- Olive oil (4 tbsp.)

The Pesto:
- Fresh basil (3 oz./80 g)
- Pine nuts (1 .75 oz./50 g)
- Cloves of garlic (3)
- Olive oil (4 - 1/16 oz./120 ml)
- Fresh parmesan (1.75 oz./50 g)

Instructions:

1. Peel and chop/dice the garlic and onion.
2. Prepare the smooth pesto paste in a blender by mixing a pinch of salt, garlic, pine nuts, and basil. Make the consistency thick when adding the oil and parmesan. Add water (2 tbsp.) if needed.
3. Warm a big skillet to heat the oil. Sauté the onion and garlic (2 min.).
4. Empty the beans into a colander to drain.
5. Add the stock and prepared vegetables to cook (12 min.). Then, mix in the drained beans and pasta to simmer until tender (6-7 min.).
6. Place the pan on a cool burner and mix in the fresh pesto.
7. Add a bit of salt, pepper, and a dusting of parmesan to enjoy promptly for the most flavorful taste.

Wine Favorites: A Sangiovese di Romagna or Chianti Classico are unquestionably the ideal wines for a minestrone.

Tomato Soup

Total Time: 45 min.
Yields Provided: 2 portions

Ingredients Used:

- Unsalted butter (4 tbsp.)
- Large onion (half of 1 – large wedges)
- Tomatoes – whole - peeled or crushed (28 oz. can)
- Water or veggie stock – low-sodium (1.5 cups)
- Salt – fine sea (.5 tsp./as desired)
- Suggested: Immersion blender

Instructions:

1. Melt butter using a medium temperature setting in a large saucepan.
   Slice the onion into wedges and combine with water, can of tomatoes with juices, and salt (.5 tsp.) Wait for it to come to a simmer with the lid off (40 min.).
2. Stir infrequently – adding salt to taste. Blend to the desired texture.
3. *Note:* You should blend in batches if using a regular blender.

Wine Favorites: A medium-bodied red wine, such as Chianti, would go well. Chianti is a terrific wine to pair with foods that contain tomatoes since it has aromas of red fruit, a bit of earth, and sparkling acidity. Another good option is Merlot, a medium-bodied red wine with overtones of cherry and plum.

Chapter 2: Italian Pasta Favorites

You may have your private list for pasta and wine; Do you have these?

Wine Favorites for Pasta:

- Pinot Noir is renowned for its rich and earthy undertones.
- Riesling is a lighter red wine.
- Merlot is a grape wine option with a deep blue color that can be utilized to make both blended wines and varietal wines.
- Cabernet Sauvignon - The international red wine grape variety of the same name is used to produce the full-bodied, acidic wine. Strong tannins that mature well are present. The average alcohol content of Cabernet Sauvignon wines is between 13 and 14 percent.
- Zinfandel - Another sweet red wine choice is Zinfandel. Wines made from this delicious Croatian grape have flavors reminiscent of strawberries, canned peaches, and sweet tobacco. Malbec ranks highly on the red wine sweetness scale even though it is not by any means a sweet wine.

Now, let us Begin!

Almond Spaghetti

Total Time: 25 min.
Yields Provided: 4 portions

Ingredients Used:

- Barilla spaghetti (350 g)
- Noberasco - organic almonds (10 - shelled)
- Garlic (1 clove)
- Lemon juice (from 1 lemon)
- Lemon grated zest (2 lemons)
- Hot chili pepper (1)
- Olive oil
- Salt
- Parsley (1 bunch)

Instructions:

1. Prepare the almonds in a skillet of hot oil. During the browning process, scoot them around, drain, and discard the skin while breaking them into small bits.
2. Mince and add the hot pepper and garlic to sauté (the same pan is okay).
3. Prepare a pot of water with salt to prepare the spaghetti; drain them when they are al dente. Toss them into the skillet with the dressing.
4. Place the pan on a cool burner. Prepare the lemon for juice and zest to combine with the almonds and freshly chopped parsley.
5. Toss gently and plate to serve.

Wine Favorites: Have a glass of Chardonnay or Chardonnay Sicilia DOC

Black Fusilli with Hazelnuts & Leek

Total Time: 35 min.
Yields Provided: 2 portions

Ingredients Used:

- Large sepia fusilli/pasta (140 g)
- Toasted - organic hazelnuts (40 g)
- Leek (1 large)
- Parmalat - Zymil milk (1 glass/as needed)
- Hard ricotta/Auricchio pecorino cheese
- Olive oil
- Salt & black pepper
- Suggested: Non-stick skillet

Instructions:

1. Wash and thinly slice the leek.
2. Coarsely chop the hazelnuts – leaving several of them whole.
3. Warm the skillet using a high temperature setting. Toast the hazelnuts until they have released their aroma.
4. Toss and stir in the leek, lower the heat, add a spoonful of oil, and a couple pinches of salt and pepper. Once browning, stir in the milk, place a top, and simmer ten minutes.
5. Extinguish the heat and keep covered.
6. Cook the fusilli in hot salted water and drain them 'al dente'.
7. Toss them in the skillet with the leek and milk dressing to sauté (2 min.)
8. Top the dishes with grated cheese and serve immediately.

Note: Fusilli are a variety of pasta that are formed into corkscrew or helical shapes.

Wine Favorites: Smooth dry white wines such as Chenin Blanc and subtle oaked Chardonnay. Italian whites such as Gavi or Soave could also be a favorite option.

Bucatini all'Amatriciana

Total Time: 40 min.
Yields Provided: 8 portions

Ingredients Used:

- Extra-virgin olive oil (2 tbsp.)
- Pancetta or guanciale, diced into tiny cubes (6 oz.)
- Yellow onion (1 small/1 cup)
- Garlic (2 cloves/2 tsp.)
- San Marzano tomatoes (28 oz.)
- Dry white wine (.33 or 1/3 cup)
- Red pepper flakes (.25 tsp./to your liking)
- Freshly ground black pepper & salt (to your liking)
- Dry bucatini pasta (16 oz.)
- Pecorino Romano cheese (.75 cup)
- Optional to Garnish: Parsley (2 tbsp.)
- Also Needed: 12-inch sauté pan

Instructions:

1. Dice the pancetta and onions into ¼-inch cubes. Mince the garlic and onions.
2. Finely crush the tomatoes with your hands. Lastly, mince/dice the parsley and shred the cheese.
3. Prepare a big pot of water to boil.
4. Heat the oil using a medium temperature setting. When heated, add the pancetta to sauté till it is golden brown (5 min.). Transfer to a plate while leaving fat in the pan.
5. Now add and sauté the onions (3 min.), then toss in the garlic and continue sautéing (20 sec.).
6. Mix in the wine, tomatoes, pepper flakes, cooked pancetta, and pepper.
7. Wait for it to simmer - adjust the temperature setting to low and simmer with the lid off the pot (15-20 min.).
8. In the meantime, prepare the pasta in lightly salted water (.5 tsp). Drain the pasta.
9. Toss the pasta with the finished sauce and the Romano cheese.
10. Taste for salt and serve right away, garnished with parsley.

Wine Favorites: You can enjoy a red grape Montepulciano d'Abruzzo and the white grape Pecorino with this dish.

Cannelloni with Asparagus

Total Time: 50 min.
Yields Provided: 4 portions

Ingredients Used:

- Barilla cannelloni (10)
- Ricotta (350 g)
- Green asparagus (200 g)
- Auricchio mozzarella (200 g)
- Scallion (1)
- Parmareggio – 30-month-old Parmigiano Reggiano (as desired)
- Béchamel sauce
- Cirio passata
- Olive oil
- Salt and pepper

Instructions:

1. Dice the scallion and grate the mozzarella. Prepare the asparagus into 2-3 cm/0.78 to 1.2-inch-pieces.
2. Toss the scallion with the asparagus to sauté (5 min.). Cool and mix in the ricotta, mozzarella, pepper, and salt.
3. Add salt to a pot of water to boil the cannelloni (2 min.).
4. Fill a pastry bag with the asparagus mixture and pipe inside each cannelloni.
5. Use a saucepan to prepare the passata sauce with the remaining chopped scallion and olive oil (10 min.).
6. Arrange the filled cannelloni in a baking tray, cover with the sauce, and a dusting of grated cheese over its top.
7. Bake in the oven at 356° Fahrenheit or 180° Celsius (10 min.).
8. Serve with the sauce.

Wine Favorites: Sangiovese, Barbera, Dolcetto, and Valpolicella Classico. Italian white wines such as Trebbiano, Fiano, and Soave will be excellent with your Cannelloni. Or grab a bottle of Pinot Grigio, Zinfandel, or sparkling wine.

Cavatelli with Broccoli

Total Time: 25 min.
Yields Provided: 4 portions

Ingredients Used:

- Homemade cavatelli/pasta (1 lb.)
- Broccoli (2 lb.)
- Garlic (4 cloves)
- Pepperoncino
- Olive oil

Instructions:

1. Prepare a big pot with salted water.
2. Toss in the broccoli to boil (10 min.).
3. Next, mix in the pasta and simmer till they are al dente.
4. Drain the pasta and broccoli - leaving behind two cups of water in them.
5. Prepare a sauté pan with six tablespoons of oil and make it hot. Add the garlic and the pepperoncino.
6. Once the garlic is lightly browned, pour the oil and the garlic over the cavatelli.
7. Mix and serve.

Wine Favorites: Most United States imports from the Cerasuolo di Vittoria DOC are outstanding. Sicilian reds, particularly - Nero d'Avola and Cerasuolo di Vittoria - including Passopisciaro, Calabretta, Santa Anastasia , and Occhipinti.

Linguine in Bell Pepper Cream Sauce

Total Time: 30 min.
Yields Provided: 4 portions

Ingredients Used:

- Barilla Linguine/Giovanni Rana Spaghetti (320 g)
- Tomatoes (4 plum)
- Red bell pepper (a large ripe)
- Cream/ Valsoia Condisoia/another favorite (40 ml/4 tbsp.)
- Olive oil (20 g/2 tbsp)
- Salt
- Suggested: Non-stick pan-

Instructions:

1. Thoroughly rinse, clean, and dice the peppers and tomatoes.
2. Toss them into the pan with oil and simmer - adding salt as desired (10 min.).
3. Place it on the countertop to combine using a hand blender.
4. Mix in the cream with the sauce and add to the pan to simmer (5 min.).
5. Prepare a pot of boiling salted water to cook the pasta, drain, and mix in with the sauce.

Wine Favorites: Enjoy your treat with one of these special wine options:

- Rocca di Montemassi Calasole Vermentino Maremma Toscana DOC
- Zonin Montepulciano d'Abruzzo DOC
- Santa Margherita Chianti Classico DOCG

Pasta with Peas - Pasta e Piselli

Total Time: 55-60 min.
Yields Provided: 4 portions

Ingredients Used:

- Water (2 quarts - to start)
- Onion (1 large)
- Salt (2 tsp.)
- Olive oil (3 tbsp.)
- Frozen peas (10 oz. bag)
- Fresh parsley (1 pinch/as desired)
- Dried baby shell pasta/ditalini (1 lb.)
- Pecorino Romano cheese (as desired)

Instructions:

1. Use a medium temperature setting to heat the water to boiling with salt.
2. Dice and toss in the onion (¼-inch dice), salt, and oil to the pan. Simmer till the onion softened (1/2 hr.).
3. Add the peas and continue simmering (15-20 min.) with a portion of parsley.
4. Now, add the pasta to the pot of heated water to cook (1/2 of the pkg. time for al dente). Drain and add it to the peas.
5. Thoroughly toss and serve with a sprinkle of grated cheese.

Wine Favorites: The peas' perky, fresh green flavor, coupled with the lightness of this dish, means Bianco and Rosato wines work best.

Pennette alla Puttanesca

Total Time: 40 min.
Yields Provided: 4 portions

Ingredients Used:

- Penne noodles (320 g/.75 lb.)
- Peeled tomatoes (800 g/1.75 lb.)
- Anchovies in oil (1 oz./25 g)
- Salted capers (.33 or 1/3 oz./10 g)
- Parsley (1 bunch)
- Gaeta olives ½ cup (.5 cup/100 g)
- Garlic (3 cloves)
- Dried chili pepper (2)
- Extra-virgin olive oil (2.5 tbsp./30 g)
- Fine salt (as desired)

Instructions:

1. First rinse the capers under running water to remove the excess salt, then dry them and chop them into chunks with a knife. Pit and crush the olives by pushing down with the blade of a knife.
2. Wash, dry, and chop the parsley.
3. Make a soup pot of water for the pasta with salt – wait for it to boil.
4. In the meantime, add the oil, whole peeled garlic cloves, chopped dried chili, and anchovies to a large frying pan.
5. Rinse and add the capers to sauté using a medium temperature setting till the anchovies have dissolved and released aromas.
6. Next, mash the peeled tomatoes slightly and add them to the pan while stirring using medium heat (10 min.)
7. Meanwhile, cook the penne until it is al dente.
8. When the sauce is ready, mix in the garlic, crushed olives, and chopped parsley.
9. Now drain the pasta and pour directly into the pan, flipping it for 30 seconds, just enough time to allow all the flavors to meld together.
10. Serve it promptly for the most flavorful results.

Wine Favorites: Pasta Puttanesca pairs best acidic and earthy notes red wines like Pinot Noir, Chianti Classico, Primitivo, Beaujolais Cru, Barbera, and Nero d'Avola.

Rigatoni alla Papino

Total Time: 30-35 min.
Yields Provided: 4 portions

Ingredients Used:

- Rigatoni pasta (1 lb.)
- Olive oil (3 tbsp.)
- Garlic (4 cloves)
- Mixed ground meat - pork, veal & beef (1 lb.)
- Sage (4 leaves)
- Bay leaves (2)
- Red wine (.5 cup)
- Salt
- Red pepper flakes
- Tomato paste (3 oz.)

Instructions:

1. First, prepare a soup pot with salted water, wait for it to boil, and add the rigatoni.
2. Prep a sauté pan with oil. Mince and toss in the garlic to sauté several minutes till it turns lightly golden. Now mix in the ground meat.
3. Sauté it while breaking it apart with a wooden spoon.
4. Add the sage and bay leaves - crushed by hand - while adding pepper flakes and salt to your liking.
5. Sauté the meat until it turns brown and mix in the wine. Simmer for a short time, then add the tomato paste.
6. Set the temperature setting to low, add two tablespoons of pasta water, and cover the pan. Simmer, adding water as needed (10 min.).
7. Once the noodles are al dente, pour them into the sauce, and toss for 1 minute until the Rigatoni are well coated with the sauce (1 min.).
8. Serve with a portion of cheese as desired.

Wine Favorites: Try pairing this delicious meal with Chianti Classico, Beaujolais Cru, or Primitivo.

Seaweed Spaghetti with Clams & Vinegar

Total Time: 45 min.
Yields Provided: 4 portions

Ingredients Used:

- Spaghetti - Barilla used (280 g)
- Clams (500 g)
- White wine (10 ml)
- Filippo Berio - olive oil (5 ml)
- White wine vinegar - Ponti lemon flavor used (3 tbsp.)
- Garlic (1 clove)
- Laurel/bay leaf
- Salt

Instructions:

1. Prepare the spaghetti in a pot of boiling salted water, drain, and let it cool.
2. Open the clams separately.
3. Add oil to a skillet to sauté the garlic, bay leaves, and clams (still in the shells), white wine, and cover with a lid.
4. Once they are ready, remove the clams from the shell, and reserve the water for later.
5. Prepare a vinaigrette by mixing the saved water, vinegar, and oil. Serve the clams and the vinaigrette over the spaghetti, toss thoroughly, and enjoy.

Wine Favorites: Friulano Friuli Aquileia DOC Superiore is a favored choice.

Spaghetti alla Carbonara

Total Time: 35 min.
Yields Provided: 4-6 portions

Ingredients Used:

- Dry spaghetti (1 lb.)
- Olive oil (2 tbsp.)
- Pancetta/slab bacon (4 oz.)
- Garlic (4 cloves)
- Eggs (2 large)
- Freshly grated Parmigiano-Reggiano (1 cup + more to serve)
- Black pepper
- Fresh flat-leaf parsley (1 scoop/as desired)

Instructions:

1. Prepare a big pot of salted water. Once boiling, toss in the pasta to cook till it is al dente (8-10 min.)
2. Thoroughly drain the pasta (setting aside 0.5 cup for the sauce).
3. In the meantime, warm oil in a deep skillet using a medium temperature setting. Slice the meat into strips or cubes and add to the pan to sauté till the fat is rendered and it is crispy (3 min.).
4. Mince, add, and sauté the garlic (just under a min.).
5. Drain and add the spaghetti to the pan while tossing it in the fat (2 min.).
6. Whisk the eggs with the parmesan in a mixing container.
7. Place the pan on the countertop and briskly whisk in the egg-cheese mixture to the pasta till thickened – not scrambled.
8. Use the 'saved' water (step 2) to thin the sauce till it is as you like it. Then add a dusting of pepper and salt.
9. Scoop the delicious meal into warm serving bowls with a garnishing of chopped parsley with cheese optionally served on the side.

Wine Favorites: Pinot Grigio and Gavi would be the ideal mate. However, if you utterly had to have a red, try for a fresh Montepulciano.

Spaghetti Cacio e Pepe

Total Time: 20 min.
Yields Provided: 4 portions

Ingredients Used:

- Spaghetti (1 lb.)
- Olive oil (6 tbsp.)
- Garlic cloves (2)
- Black pepper (2 tsp.)
- Grated Pecorino Romano cheese (1.75 cups)

Instructions:

1. Prepare the spaghetti in a soup pot with lightly salted water until tender - yet firm (12 min.). Reserve one cup of cooking water, then drain the cooked spaghetti.
2. Use a medium heat setting to warm oil in a big frying pan.
3. Mince and sauté the pepper and garlic in hot oil until fragrant (1-2 min.).
4. Add the prepared spaghetti and cheese with one-half cup reserved cooking water – stirring till the cheese is gooey (1 min.).
5. Stir in more cooking water as needed, one tablespoon at a time, till the sauce coats the spaghetti (1 min.).

Wine Favorites: You can enjoy your favorite dish with the following beverages (suggestions included):

- Cabernet Sauvignon –ONEHOPE California Cabernet Sauvignon.
- Chianti –Bell'Agio Chianti.
- Pinot Grigio –Santa Margherita Pinot Grigio.
- Riesling –Empire Estate Dry Reisling.
- Pinot Noir – sFEL Pinot Noir Anderson Valley.

Tomato & Aubergine Lasagne

Total Time: 1 hr. 15 min.
Yields Provided: 4 portions

Ingredients Used:

- Barilla Lasagna (1 pkg.)
- Eggplant/aubergines (2)
- Cirio Passata Classica (2 bottles)
- Parmigiano Reggiano - grated
- Olive oil (5 tbsp.)
- Parmalat béchamel sauce
- Black pepper
- Onion (1)
- Fresh basil
- Salt

Instructions:

1. Enjoy this as desired.
2. First, slice the eggplant (½-cm thickness) and sauté in a pan for two to three minutes.
3. Add oil to a skillet with the finely chopped onion to sauté till they are browned.
4. Mix in the sauce and season with pepper and salt; simmer till it is to your liking.
5. Spritz a baking tray with oil and create alternate layers of the lasagna with the tomato sauce, eggplant, and béchamel sauce.
6. Top with sauce and a cheese dusting.
7. Bake it at 392° Fahrenheit or 200° Celsius (20-25 min.).
8. Wait about ten minutes to serve with a garnishing of fresh basil leaves.

Wine Favorites: Choose from one of these:

- Chianti Classico Riserva DOCG
- Zonin Valpolicella DOC

Chapter 3: Italian Polenta Favorites

Let us see what delicious wine partners polenta has in store for your dining pleasure!

The Favorite Accompaniments:

Red wine

- Nobile di Montepulciano
- Chianti

Rosso Di Montalcino

White Wines:

- Pinot Grigio
- Chardonnay

Baccala Mantecato

Total Time: 60 min.
Yields Provided: 6 portions

Ingredients Used:

- Instant polenta (7 1/16 oz./200 g)
- Salted cod fillet or stockfish - pre-soaked (1.33/1-1/3 lb./600 g)
- Milk (2.125 or 2-1/8 pints)
- Black peppercorns (10)
- Bay leaf (1)
- Olive oil (.5 pint/250 ml)
- Black pepper & salt
- For Serving: Freshly chopped parsley

Instructions:

1. Prepare the polenta per the manufacturer's directions. Spread it over a baking tray covered with a layer of parchment paper. Put a layer over the top, followed by another baking tray. Now, push and add a heavy saucepan on top and wait for it to cool.
2. Prepare a saucepan to boil with the fish, milk, bay leaf, and peppercorns to gently simmer (10 min.). Cover them and wait for ten minutes.
3. Now, trim the fish while mashing it till it is flaky.
4. Toss the fish into a food processor with milk (2–3 tbsp.) and pulse it into a paste.
5. Use a low-speed setting to add the oil - little by little - till the mixture has a light and fluffy consistency.
6. Adjust seasonings, cool, garnish with a little parsley, and store in the fridge till it is serving time.
7. Slice the polenta into rectangles (2x4-inches) and toast each side to serve (1 per serving).

Wine Favorites: Enjoy with a glass of Prosecco della Valdobbiadene.

Broccoli & Polenta

Total Time: 1 hr. 30 min.
Yields Provided: Portions vary

Ingredients Used:

- Olive oil (as needed)
- Corn flour for polenta (180 g)
- Water (900 ml/30.4 oz.)
- Goat cheese (120 g)
- Broccoli (200 g)
- Pine nuts (4 tbsp.)
- Poppy seeds (2 tbsp.)
- Fresh parsley
- Black pepper and salt

Instructions:

1. Prep a pot of water with salt and wait for it to boil. Lower the heat setting and whisk in the flour - briskly mixing to avoid lumps (50 min.). Add boiling water as needed.
2. Thoroughly wash the broccoli and stir fry in a saucepan with oil (1 tbsp.), pepper, and salt (5 min.).
3. Prepare another skillet to toast the pine nuts.
4. Once the polenta is cooked, add the goat's cheese, and mix with a sprinkle of pepper as desired.
5. Pour the polenta into four bowls and add the broccoli and the pine nuts.
6. Serve with a portion of freshly chopped parsley and poppy seeds.

Wine Favorites: Serve the dish with Chardonnay or Rosso di Montalcino.

Chicken with Mushroom & Polenta

Total Time: 1 hr. 25 min.
Yields Provided: 4 portions

Ingredients Used:

- Chicken (1)
- Cornmeal (2 cups)
- Champignon mushrooms (3 cups)
- Butter
- Salami
- Dry white wine
- Dried porcini mushrooms (8 pieces)
- Garlic (1 clove)
- Minced parsley
- White onion (1)
- Vegetable broth
- Olive oil
- Pepper & salt (as desired)

Instructions:

1. Prepare a container of warm water to soak the dried mushrooms.
2. Clean and slice the champignons.
3. Thoroughly rinse the chicken and portion it into eight pieces. Thoroughly wash and mince the giblets.
4. Fry the chicken in a skillet with the butter, pepper, and salt (6-7 min.).
5. Transfer the chicken from the pan to a dish.
6. Sauté the sliced onion, the garlic clove (peel attached & crushed), and 1 tablespoon minced parsley.
7. Add the chicken to the pan with a splatter of wine – letting it evaporate (3-4 min.).
8. Then add the giblets, soaked mushrooms, minced salami, and a ladle of broth - continue to cook (45 min.).
9. Finally, add the champignons to simmer (5 min.). Remove the pan from the burner and mix in the minced parsley (2 tbsp.).
10. Next, boil six cups of water with a bit of salt and a spritz of oil.
11. Gradually, whisk in the cornmeal. Simmer the mixture for 40 to 45 minutes, whisking often.
12. Add the prepared polenta to a serving platter with the chicken and sauce to serve right away.

Wine Favorites: Pinot Grigio is great with Italian food. It is tart and crisp, perfect for cleaning your palate after a mouthful of polenta and creamy sauce.

Crunchy Polenta with Peas & Asparagus

Total Time: 60 min.
Yields Provided: 4 portions

Ingredients Used:

The Polenta:
- Stone-ground polenta flour, stone ground (7-1/16 oz.)
- Semolina flour (10.66 or 10-2/3 oz.)
- Eggs (5 whisked)

The Asparagus Filling:
- White asparagus (7-1/16 oz.)
- Asparagus (3.5 oz.)
- Onion (1)
- Peas (1.75 oz.)
- White wine (6 oz.)
- Milk
- Olive oil
- Salt & pepper

The Pea Cream:
- Olive oil
- Shallot (1)
- Peas (3.5 oz.)
- Onion (1)
- Vegetable stock (1.66 or 1-2/3 oz.)
- Pepper and salt

For Serving:
- Asparagus (half of 1 bunch)
- White asparagus (half of 1 bunch)

Instructions:

1. First, prepare the polenta dough in a big mixing container. Combine the polenta and semolina flours till they are thoroughly mixed. Spoon a well in the center of the mixture. Then, gradually mix in the egg till the mixture creates a dough.
2. Knead the dough to obtain a silky consistency. Wrap the prepared dough in cling film. Pop it in the fridge (30 min.).
3. Dice the onion and shallot.
4. Prepare a pot of water with salt and wait for it to boil. Simmer the peas until tender (2 min.). Empty the peas into a colander.
5. Measure out the filling for the asparagus (1.75 oz.), placing the rest of the peas to the side for now.
6. For the asparagus filling and heat a skillet using medium heat.

7. Add the onion to sauté in a little oil until tender. Thinly slice the asparagus and add to fry.
8. Next, deglaze the pan with wine and toss in the prepared peas.
9. Mix in enough milk to acquire a sauce-like consistency. Keep it warm till serving time.
10. Prepare the pea cream by sautéing the shallot and onion in oil. Mix in the veggie stock, pepper, salt, and prepared peas to simmer (2 min.).
11. Scoop the prepared mixture into a blender to create a velvety purée (add vegetable stock or water if needed). Keep it warm for now.
12. Remove the prepared dough from the refrigerator. Roll it out, slicing it into 16 to 20 squares (6 x 2-3/4-in.). Place them on a cookie sheet.
13. Prepare the squares under a hot grill to cook till crispy and beginning to char.
14. Meanwhile, slice the white and green asparagus in half - lengthways and again widthways - adding these to the hot grill and cooking until charred.
15. Sprinkle some of the pea cream onto each plate – then - add a crunchy polenta square.
16. Scoop a portion of asparagus filling on top of the square and cover with another square.
17. Continue the process using all the ingredients and garnish with the grilled asparagus.

Wine Favorites: Enjoy a Burgundy Chardonnay, Argentinian Malbec, or Chilean Sauvignon Blanc as a delicious enhancer for your meal.

Polenta Medallion in Tomato Sauce

Total Time: 40 min.
Yields Provided: 4-5 portions

Ingredients Used:

- Water (1,5 liters)
- Garlic (2 cloves)
- Butter (1 tbsp.)
- Polenta Valsugana - instant corn flour (350 g)
- Olive oil (4 tbsp.)
- Parmareggio - Parmigiano Reggiano - grated (50 g)
- Chopped tomatoes – Cirio used (600 g)
- Salt

Instructions:

1. Prepare a skillet with oil to heat. Sauté the minced garlic until lightly browned and add the tomatoes. Simmer with a pinch of salt (15-20 min.)
2. Prepare a saucepan with salted water. Add the flour in small portions using a whisk.
3. Simmer and stir to help the mixture from sticking (8 min.). Now, add the butter and stir.
4. Serve the polenta in individual bowls with sauce and a dusting of tasty cheese.

Wine Favorites: Try one of these delicious drinks for your first course:

- Astraio Viognier Maremma Toscana DOC
- Vernaccia di San Gimignano La Gentilesca DOCG
- Sangiovese DOC Maremma Toscana
- Dolcetto Monferrato DOC

Chapter 4: Italian Risotto

Asparagus Risotto

Total Time: 30 min.
Yields Provided: 4 portions

Ingredients Used:

- Riso Gallo - Risotto rice (340 g)
- Asparagus (300 g)
- Vegetable or chicken stock- heated (1.2 liters)
- Parmigiano Reggiano - grated (100 g)
- Onion (1 medium)
- Dry white wine (1 glass/as desired)
- Butter (40 g)

Instructions:

1. Finely chop the onion and asparagus.
2. Sauté the onion and asparagus stalks in butter until softened.
3. Add rice and coat until translucent. Stir in the wine and simmer the mixture to reduce.
4. Add the chosen stock and simmer, stirring a few times (14 min.).
5. Two minutes before the rice is cooked, gently fold in the asparagus tips.
6. Grate and mix in the parmesan to serve.

Wine Favorites: Choose from one of the following delicious wine options:

- Zonin Soave DOC
- Santa Margherita Pinot Grigio Valdadige
- Tenuta Cà Bolani Traminer Friuli Aquileia DOC Superiore
- Tenuta Cà Bolani Sauvignon Friuli Aquileia DOC Superiore

Asparagus & Anchovies Risotto

Total Time: 35 min.
Yields Provided: 4 portions

Ingredients Used:

- Asparagus (2 bunches)
- Preserved anchovies (10)
- Riso Gallo Carnaroli Gran Riserva rice (320 g)
- Parmesan cheese (50 g - grated)
- White onion (half of 1)
- Dry white wine (half of 1 glass/as desired)
- Butter
- Olive oil
- White pepper - freshly ground
- Salt

Instructions:

1. Trim the asparagus stem using a peeler and eliminate its rough stem. Chop the stems into chunks to boil in salted water (10 min.).
2. Drain the asparagus stems (saving the water). Then use a hand blender to work them into a cream.
3. Boil the asparagus tips in broth (5 min.), drain, and set aside for now.
4. Finely dice the onion, fry it in a pot with two spoons of oil, and a shake of salt.
5. Stir in the rice to toast in the mixture, stirring frequently (3 min.).
6. Drizzle in the wine and gently simmer to reduce, also adding the water (step 2).
7. Halfway through the cooking cycle, mix in the cream made with the asparagus stems, immediately followed by the asparagus tips.
8. Next, chop the anchovies and mix half of them with butter (40 g) and gently melt the others with the additional butter.
9. Add the butter mixed with the anchovies, pepper, salt, and parmesan to the risotto till it is velvety.
10. Serve the risotto with a portion of the delicious butter.

Wine Favorites: Choose Pinot grigio, Riesling Italico dell' Oltrepò for this dish.

Black Rice with River Crayfish

Total Time: 55 min.
Yields Provided: 4 portions

Ingredients Used:

- Riso Gallo Venere rice (240 g)
- River crayfish (44 large)
- Shallot (1)
- Garlic (1 clove)
- Olive oil (120 g)
- Butter (100 g)
- Parmareggio - Parmigiano Reggiano (60 g)
- Watercress (1 bunch)
- Carrot (1)
- Onion (1 small)
- Celery stick (1)
- Cirio - tomato concentrate (15 g)
- Fresh cream (20 g)
- Aromatic white wine (100 ml)

Instructions:

1. Finely chop the garlic and shallot. Grate the cheese.
2. Prepare a pot of boiling – salted water.
3. Toss the crayfish to cook (1 min.).
4. Reserve about one liter of water. Dump the crayfish into a colander to drain and then into a container of ice water. Remove its shell and vein.
5. Make four raviolis from the pasta mixture - filling each one with three lightly seasoned crayfish tails.
6. Warm oil (60 g) to sauté the onion, celery, and carrots till they are nicely browned to a light golden shade, then mix in the prawns. Add and simmer the wine till it evaporates. Next, mix in about one liter of water with the lid off till the liquids are reduced to 250 ml.
7. Pass it through a sieve to thoroughly press. Then, add the tomato concentrate and cream. Adjust seasoning and reduce slightly further.
8. Warm the remainder of the oil in a heavy-based pan to sauté and brown the shallot and garlic.
9. Mix in the rice and continue to cook – adding the crayfish water as needed.
10. When the risotto is ready, place it on a cool burner, and mix till it is velvety with the butter, cheese, and diced crayfish tails (set eight aside for decoration), then tweak the seasoning as desired.
11. Drain the ravioli and place in the crayfish liqueur.
12. Serve the risotto in individual dishes garnished with a ravioli, two crayfish, and a cress sprig on top.
13. Drizzle the crayfish liqueur around the risotto and serve promptly for a delightful dish.

Wine Favorites: Choose either Soave DOC *or* Chardonnay Poggio alle Fate Toscana IGT

Courgetti Flowers, Asparagus & Saffron Risotto

Total Time: 20 min.
Yields Provided: 4 portions

Ingredients Used:

- Gran Gallo Arborio Risotto rice (240 g)
- Parmigiano Reggiano (100 g - grated)
- Butter (30 g butter
- Extra-virgin olive oil - Filippo Berio used (4 tbsp.)
- Onion (1 chopped)
- Champagne (250 g)
- Chicken stock (2 liters)
- Zucchini/courgette flowers (10)
- Asparagus (12)
- Saffron service cup (1)
- Suggested: Heavy-bottomed saucepan

Instructions:

1. Chop, add oil, and sauté the onion in the saucepan until softened.
2. Add the rice and fry fully till it is transparent.
3. Stir in the champagne and wait for it to reduce.
4. Remove the tips (boil 5 min.), chop, and mix in the asparagus with a ladle of hot stock (as needed). Continue to simmer (16 min.).
5. Add the chopped zucchini and saffron to the risotto along with cheese and butter.
6. Portion the risotto between four serving dishes and top it with asparagus tips.

Wine Favorites: Choose from Pinot Grigio delle Venezie IGT or Sauvignon Friuli Aquileia DOC Superiore.

Lemon Risotto with Rocket & Langoustines/Lobster

Total Time: 50 min. (+) 1 hr. stock cooking time
Yields Provided: 4 portions

Ingredients Used:

- Riso Gallo Riserva 1856 - Carnaroli rice (300 g)
- Olive oil (100 ml)
- Shallot and onions (70 g)
- Lemons (2)
- Homemade - Beurre Blanc (1 tbsp.)
- Salt (to taste)
- Parsley (several leaves)
- Plum tomato (1)
- Small - live langoustines (1 kg/2.2 lb.)
- Langoustine stock (1 liter) *
- Wild rocket salad (2 bunches)
- White wine (2-3 tbsp.)
- Vecchia Romagna Brandy (1 tbsp.)
- Fresh garlic

Instructions:

1. Chop and sauté the shallots and onions in a skillet with a little olive oil.
2. Toss in the rice while stirring to toast it. Mix in the wine and simmer to reduce.
3. Prepare the stock using the heads of the shellfish. Pour in boiling langoustine stock and salt (as desired).
4. Use a high temperature setting as you add the stock, then mix in two tablespoons of tomato sauce.
5. The rice should be al dente in approximately 18 to 20 minutes. During the last three to four minutes of the cooking cycle, grate and toss in the lemon zest.
6. Quickly pan-fry the freshly shelled langoustine tails with oil, a touch of garlic, and a spritz or so of brandy.
7. Add the langoustine to the risotto, stirring continuously for a few seconds, and transfer it to a cool spot.
8. Add the Beurre Blanc, the leftover oil, a portion of lemon juice, freshly chopped parsley, rocket leaves, several peeled slivers of tomatoes, fresh pepper, and salt to the risotto - stirring until the rice consistency is creamy.
9. Place on warm plates with a garnish of langoustine tails, rocket leaves, and a drop of olive oil.
10. Enjoy it piping hot.
11. *Note*: According to the pros, langoustine is more complex and maintains a delicate taste/superior to lobster.

Wine Favorites: Choose from one of these delicious favorites:

- Santa Margherita Pinot Grigio Valdadige
- Tenuta Cà Bolani Pinot Grigio Friuli Aquileia DOC Superiore

- Zonin Insolia Chardonnay Terre Siciliane IGT
- Zonin Prosecco DOC Spumante Extra Dry

Mussel – Tomato & Oregano Risotto

Total Time: 50 min.
Yields Provided: 4 portions

Ingredients Used:

- Arborio Risotto rice - Gran Gallo (300 g)
- Mussels with shell (2 kg/4.4 lb.)
- White wine & water (1 glass/as desired)
- Garlic (1 clove)
- Organic chili (1)
- Tomatoes (2)
- Extra virgin olive oil (20 g)
- Fresh basil - parsley & oregano leaves
- Suggested to Use: Heavy-bottomed saucepan

Instructions:

1. Thoroughly wash the mussels. Prepare a heavy skillet with half of the wine and water (medium-high temperature) to simmer till the shells have opened (lid on).
2. Work the mussels out of the shells, trashing the ones that did not open properly. Sieve the liquid and set it to the side for now
3. Chop and sauté the chili and garlic in oil in the chosen pan.
4. Chop the muscles and add them along with the rice, frying till they are transparent. Mix in the remaining wine and reduce.
5. Add a ladle of heated stock and simmer. As the stock is absorbed, add more stock as needed (16 min.).
6. Chop and add the tomatoes. Then prepare it to serve with freshly chopped parsley, oregano, and basil.

Wine Favorites: Enjoy your risotto with one of these options:

- Rocca di Montemassi Calasole Vermentino Maremma Toscana DOC
- Tenuta Cà Bolani Pinot Grigio Friuli Aquileia DOC Superiore
- Zonin Prosecco DOC Spumante Extra Dry

Pumpkin & Prawn Risotto

Total Time: 40 min.
Yields Provided: 4 portions

Ingredients Used:

- Gran Gallo Arborio Risotto rice (200 g)
- Pumpkin (300 g)
- Prawns (20 jumbo)
- Butter (80 g)
- Onion (1 chopped)
- Heated beef/vegetable stock (1 liter/as needed)
- Parmareggio - Parmigiano Reggiano (1 tbsp. - grated)
- Olive oil
- Black pepper & salt (as desired)

Instructions:

1. Chop/dice and steam the pumpkin till it is softened.
2. Warm a heavy bottomed saucepan to sauté half of the chopped onion in butter (40 g) until softened. Mix in the pumpkin and continue stirring several minutes before removing it and dumping it into a sieve.
3. Shell all the prawns but four.
4. Fry the rest of the chopped onion in the remainder of the butter in a heavy bottomed saucepan until softened. Stir in the rice and sauté until transparent.
5. Add a soup spoon of the heated stock - simmer for several minutes - mix in the pumpkin cream and prawns. Add more stock as required (16 min.).
6. Remove the risotto from the heat and stir in the butter and cheese with seasonings as desired.
7. Now fry the last four prawns (2 min.).
8. When ready, serve the rice with a prawn on top.

Wine Favorites: Sauvignon Blanc, Pinot grigio or Soave are excellent options for your selection.

Truffle Risotto

Total Time: 30 min.
Yields Provided: 4 portions

Ingredients Used:

- Arborio Risotto rice - Riso Gallo Gran Gallo (300 g)
- Heated vegetable or chicken stock (1 liter/33,8 oz.)
- Butter (100 g)
- Parmareggio - Parmigiano Reggiano - grated (100 g)
- Truffle (40 g)
- Shallot (30 g)

Instructions:

1. Chop and sauté the shallots in a skillet with butter (70 g) till it is softened - not browned.
2. Mix in the rice, stir, and simmer (2-3 min.).
3. Add a ladleful of the boiling stock and continue to stir, adding more as needed till it is al dente (16 min.).
4. Place the pan on a cool burner. Stir in the remainder of the butter and grated parmesan. Wait about two minutes before serving with a garnishing of sliced truffle.

Wine Favorites: Barolo is deemed the perfect wine for pairing with this dish.

Chapter 5: Salad Favorites

Try a delicious salad for your first course!

Barley Salad with Tuna & Grilled Veggies

Total Time: 30 min.
Yields Provided: 4 portions

Ingredients Used:

- Tuna in Brine – ex. Rio Mare (160 g pkg.)
- Pearl barley or Riso Gallo - 3 Grains - spelt – rice & barley (200 g)
- Olive oil
- Red pepper (1)
- Courgettes/zucchini (2)
- Aubergine/eggplant (1)
- Rosemary
- Salt and black pepper

Instructions:

1. Prepare a pot of water with salt to cook the barley (20 min.). Strain and rinse it under cold water, then thoroughly drain it.
2. Slice the eggplant and zucchini into thick slices and the pepper into strips. Prepare them over a hot griddle.
3. Dice the veggies and rosemary - toss with a dusting of salt and pepper.
4. Add a splash of oil and barley. Drain the tuna, slice it into chunks, and add to the mix to serve.

Wine Favorites: Choose from one of these options; Insolia Chardonnay Terre Siciliane IGT *or* Vernaccia di San Gimignano La Gentilesca DOCG.

Fig Salad

Total Time: 10 min.
Yields Provided: 4 portions

Ingredients Used:

- Rockets (2)
- Ripe figs (12 - halved)
- Grana Padano - like Parmigiano Reggiano - finely grated (30 g)
- Vinegar - white wine type used (1 tbsp.)
- Olive oil (3 tbsp.)
- Crushed pink peppercorns (1 tsp.)

Instructions:

1. Lay the rocket and figs with the cut side up on a platter.
2. Load a blender with the remainder of the fixings (except the pink peppercorns) while pulsing or use a stick blender till it is velvety smooth.
3. Lastly, mix in a splash of just boiled water - whizz again until emulsified.
4. Spoon the dressing over the figs then sprinkle with crushed peppercorns to finish.

Wine Favorites: Try a Burgundy Chardonnay white wine.

Puntarelle Salad with Capers & Anchovies

Total Time: 45 min.
Yields Provided: 6 portions

Ingredients Used:

- Puntarelle/type of chicory* (600 g)
- Garlic (12 cloves)
- Whole milk (200 ml)
- Anchovies (7-8 fillets)
- Red wine vinegar (1 tbsp.)
- To Garnish: Capers

Instructions:

1. Thinly slice the larger, hardier leaves of the chickory/punterelle using a julienne style. (The smaller ones can be eaten raw, so reserve them.).
2. Prepare a pot of lightly salted water to blanch the thicker slices (1-2 min.), then scoop into a container of ice-cold water.
3. Prepare the dressing by discarding the peel and mince the garlic cloves in a small pan. Cover with the milk, water (200 ml), and a dash of salt. Gently simmer for ½-hour, till the cloves are soft enough to be crushed with the back of a fork.
4. At that time, chop and add a few fillets of anchovies - as well as a spoonful of the oil they are preserved in, and whisk to emulsify the dressing.
5. Lastly, fully drain the puntarelle and shake off as much water as possible.
6. Add the shaved puntarelle, smaller green leaves, dressing, and a spoonful of vinegar to a mixing bowl and combine.
7. Taste for seasonings and add a few capers over the top to serve.

Note: From November to April, puntarelle, a traditional Roman starter, are available in all eateries in the city center as well as in surrounding trattorias. Escarole is a great substitute.

Wine Favorites: Despite their boldness, chicories are fundamentally leafy greens. Typically, crisp wines with grassy or herbal flavors, such Sauvignon Blanc, Verdejo, or Grüner Veltliner, are complemented with green vegetables.

Rosemary Ravioli Salad with Chicken

Total Time: 15 min.
Yields Provided: 2-3 portions

Ingredients Used:

- Roasted red peppers - Ponti used - from a jar (100 g)
- Succulent Chicken with Rosemary Ravioli - ex. Giovanni Rana (250 g pkg.)
- Large courgette/zucchili (1)
- Parma ham (4 slices)
- Mixed salad leaves (2 plentiful handfuls)
- Olive oil (4 tbsp.)
- Salt & organic black pepper (freshly ground to taste)
- For Serving: Parmareggio - Parmigiano Reggiano (shaved or grated)

Instructions:

1. Diagonally slice the zucchini into thin pieces as desired. Drain and slice the peppers.
2. Preheat a grill or griddle pan. Use half the olive oil to brush over the zucchini slices, then grill them in batches till they are tender.
3. Mix them with the roasted peppers and set aside a few minutes.
4. Meanwhile, prepare a pot of boiling water with salt added to cook the ravioli. Simmer gently (4 min.).
5. Thoroughly drain the ravioli and toss with the veggies.
6. Scoop the mixture over the lettuce. Then tear apart the ham and scatter over the leaves of salad.
7. Spritz with oil and cheese to your liking.

Wine Favorites: One of these will meld with the dish.

- Bardolino DOC
- Vernaccia di San Gimignano La Gentilesca DOCG
- Valpolicella Ripasso Superiore DOC

Sicilian Salad

Total Time: 30 min.
Yields Provided: 4-6 portions

Ingredients Used:

- Watermelon (1 small)
- Red chicory (2 small heads)
- Moscatel vinegar or white balsamic (50 ml)
- Pistachios – ex. green Iranian (65g)
- Aged pecorino - such as Sardo/an aged parmesan (150 g) cut into irregular shards
- Groundnut/peanut or arachis oil (70 ml)
- Fennel fronds/herb or dill (1 handful)

Instructions:

1. Trim the chicory by halving the larger leaves, trimming the stalks, and removing the leaves.
2. Cut the melon in half through the width and reserve half for a separate treat. Peel the other half of skin and the white pith and dice the flesh into 2-cm (0.79 inch) pieces. Toss into a mixing container with the chicory leaves, vinegar, pepper, and salt.
3. Toss the nuts into a skillet (medium temperature) to dry cook till they are fragrant and have begun to release their oil. Season generously with salt; chop into chunks to mix into the watermelon.
4. Fold in the pecorino and add the nut oil and fennel fronds.
5. Briefly mix again and serve.

Wine Favorites: Dry Oregon Pinot Gris or Alsace are great choices.

Chapter 6: Delicious Seafood Starter Options

Baked Feta with Roasted Grapes & Rosemary

Total Time: 40 min.
Yields Provided: 4 portions

Ingredients Used:

- Block of feta (200 g)
- Red grapes (200 g)
- Rosemary (2 sprigs)
- Olive oil (2 tbsp.)
- Runny honey (as desired)
- For Serving: Focaccia

Instructions:

1. Put two sheets of foil - one just larger than the other sheet - arranged over one another on a work surface.
2. Position the feta in the center and add the grapes with the rosemary (small sprigs).
3. Drizzle with the olive oil, honey, and a shake of black pepper. Scrunch the sides and seal the parcel. Chill until ready to serve (up to 1 day).
4. Warm the oven to reach 392° Fahrenheit/200° Celsius,
5. Bake until the grapes have burst, and the feta is softened (30-35 min.).
6. Serve with warmed focaccia for dunking.

Wine Favorites: Some people enjoy this dish paired with a New Zealand Sauvignon Blanc or unoaked Moschofilero.

Brown Shrimp Ranhofer

Total Time: 20 min.
Yields Provided: 4 portions

Ingredients Used:

- Unsalted butter (25 g)
- Plain flour (1 tbsp.)
- Single cream (200 ml)
- Egg (1 yolk)
- Cayenne pepper (.5 tsp. + more for serving)
- Nutmeg
- Brandy (2 tbsp.)
- Lemon - juiced (half of 1)
- Cooked brown shrimp (140 g)
- Sourdough (4 slices - toasted)

Instructions:

1. Melt the butter in a frying pan until it begins to foam. Then mix in the flour - stirring for two minutes. Slowly mix in the single cream until you have a smooth sauce.
2. Briskly whisk the egg yolk and pour over one-third of the sauce. Pour in the remaining sauce, then tip the mixture back into the pan.
3. Simmer while stirring regularly until it thickly covers the back of a spoon.
4. Mix in the nutmeg, cayenne pepper, brandy, lemon juice, and seasoning.
5. Stir in the shrimp to heat for several minutes, then pile onto sourdough toast, sprinkle with a little extra cayenne, and serve.

Wine Favorites: A hearty Chardonnay is one fabulous option, or you may enjoy a Cabernet Sauvignon.

Chili & Herb Calamari

Total Time: 35 min.
Yields Provided: 4 portions

Ingredients Used:

- Milk (50 ml)
- Plain flour (50 g)
- Corn flour (50 g)
- *To Deep-Fry*: Vegetable oil
- Cleaned squid (400 g)
- Red chili (2)
- Spring onions (3)
- Peanuts (1 handful)
- Sea salt flakes (as required)
- Coriander (half of 1 small bunch)
- Limes (2 into wedges)

Instructions:

1. Do the prep. Remove seeds and thinly slice the chili at an angle. Use the same cut on the onions. Finely chop the peanuts and coriander. Clean and slice the squid into one-cm rings.
2. Measure and add the milk into a shallow bowl - each type of flour together in another with seasoning to your taste.
3. Now, fill a pan with oil (not over one-third full). Warm till a cube of bread browns in 30 seconds (356° Fahrenheit/180° Celsius).
4. Prepare them in batches if needed. First, dip the squid into milk (letting excess drip) and dip it into the seasoned flour to fully coat.
5. Gently lower the squid into the hated oil to cook until crispy (1-2 min. in batches if needed). Scoop them onto a paper-lined platter with a dash of salt flakes.
6. Prepare the squid with spring onions, chilies, peanuts, and coriander.
7. Serve the tasty dish with a few lime wedges for added flavor.

Wine Favorites: Pinot Noir or Brute style Chardonnay are a perfect combination with sweet squid.

Garlic-Chili Clams on Sourdough Toast

Total Time: 15 min.
Yields Provided: 4 portions

Ingredients Used:

- Olive oil (6 tbsp.)
- Garlic (4 cloves)
- Red chili pepper (1)
- White wine (150 ml)
- Parma ham (3 slices - shredded)
- Cleaned clams (500 g)
- Sourdough slices - toasted (4 thick)
- Parsley – flat-leaf (half of 1 small bunch)
- Lemon (1 - wedged)

Instructions:

1. Warm the oil in a skillet to fry the ham with a top added till it is crispy.
2. Remove the chili seeds. Slice and mix in the chili and garlic. Sauté till softened (3 min.).
3. Stir in the white wine till it is bubbling. Then toss in the clams, place a top, and let them cook (5-6 min.). Shake till the clams open.
4. Arrange the toast on plates with a soup spoon of clams and the garlicky dressing.
5. Garnish the dish with finely chopped parsley and a wedge of lemon for a twangy flavor boost.

Wine Favorites: For your personal reference, you will find 'steamed' clams are most flavorful with the highly acidic Sauvignon Blanc, or a dry Rosé. However, clams prepared in 'creamy' sauce, a mid-range white - Burgundy would be tastier.

Moules Marinière

Total Time: 30 min.
Yields Provided: 4 portions

Ingredients Used:

- Butter (50 g)
- Garlic clove (1)
- Medium leeks (2 - white parts cut in half lengthwise & sliced (greens for another use)
- Dry white wine (300 ml)
- Mussels - cleaned (2 kg)
- Double cream (150 ml)
- To Serve: Flat-leaf parsley (A handful - chopped)

Instructions:

1. Prepare a shallow pan to warm the butter - top on.
2. Heat the butter in a wide, shallow, lidded pan. Chop and toss in the garlic and leeks to sauté until softened. Pour in the wine and wait for it to bubble. Now, add the mussels and cover.
3. Shake the pan until all the mussels have opened (2-3 min. & trash any unopened ones not).
4. Pour in the cream and seasoning to simmer.
5. Serve as desired with the chopped parsley.

Wine Favorites: Try a dry white wine this will go very well: a white wine from Entre-Deux-Mers in the Bordeaux region such as, A Pouilly- Fuméor aVouvray. Or choose from white wines such as Burgundy with a Chablis.

Mushroom Pâté

Total Time: 45 min.
Yields Provided: 6 portions

Ingredients Used:

- Dried porcini mushrooms (25 g)
- Chestnut mushrooms (500 g)
- Portobello mushrooms (3)
- Vegetable oil (2 tbsp.)
- Shallots (2)
- Garlic (3 cloves)
- Thyme (several sprigs)
- Dry sherry (50 ml)
- Soft cheese (250 g)
- Crushed black peppercorns (.5 tsp.)

Instructions:

1. Toss the dried mushrooms into a small heat-proof bowl and add boiling water (100 ml). Put the chestnut and portobello mushrooms into a food processor to pulse until finely chopped.
2. Warm oil (1 tbsp.) in a big skillet using a medium-high temperature. Finely chop and toss in the mushrooms with a dash of salt. Fry and toss them until the moisture has evaporated and the mushrooms are beginning to caramelize (10 min.). Add them back into the food processor.
3. Then finely chop the cloves and shallots. Strip the leaves from the thyme.
4. Warm the remainder of oil and add the shallot with a pinch of salt to fry until softened (5 min.) Then mix in the garlic and thyme leaves.
5. Simmer the mixture for a minute and add in the sherry.
6. Drain the porcini mushrooms (reserve 50ml of the liquid). Finely chop the mushrooms and add to the pan with the liquid. Simmer till the liquid has almost evaporated. Cool slightly and add to the food processor.
7. Add the soft cheese with the black pepper and whizz everything to a smooth pâté. Scrape into a serving bowl to serve.

Wine Favorites: Pinot noir or Cabernet are perfect choices for these pâtés, or try a fuller bodied wine like Zinfandel.

Namas

Total Time: 30 min.
Yields Provided: 4 portions

Ingredients Used:

- Red snapper fillet (800 g)
- Red chili (1 long)
- Coriander (1/4 of 1 bunch)
- Lime - juiced (100 ml)
- Thick coconut cream (250 ml)
- Dark soy sauce (2 tbsp.)
- Sea salt flakes (1 pinch/as desired)
- For Serving: Sweet potato or taro chips

Instructions:

1. Use a sharp knife and discard the fish skin. Finely dice the chili and snapper. Thinly slice the coriander. Squeeze the lime for juice.
2. Dice the fish into small bite-sized chunks. Toss them with the lime juice, coriander, and chilis to set aside for now (10 min.).
3. Mix in the coconut cream, sea salt, and soy sauce and sea salt. Chill in the refrigerator (15 min.).
4. Serve with a side of taro or sweet potato crisps.

Wine Favorites: Enjoy the snapper with a Chardonnay, Pinot Rigio, or Sauvignon Blanc.

Nanami Gyoza

Total Time: 60 min. (+) salting time
Yields Provided: 6 portions

Ingredients Used:

- White cabbage (350 g/about half of 1 cabbage)
- Tofu or pork mince (500 g)
- Spring onions (2)
- Garlic (2 cloves)
- Nanami chili paste (1 tbsp.)
- Round gyoza wrappers - defrosted (40-50 frozen)

- *To Fry*: Vegetable oil of choice
- *To Dip*: Soy sauce or ponzu sauce

Instructions:

1. First, defrost the gyoza wrappers. Finely shred the cabbage and onions, then crush the garlic cloves.

2. Dust the cabbage with salt (1 tsp.) while massaging it with your hands (45 sec.). Wait for about ten minutes to release some of its juices, followed by pressing the cabbage into a sieve to remove the remainder of the excess liquid.
3. Thoroughly combine the mince with the onions, cabbage, garlic, and Nanami.
4. Add a heaping teaspoon of the filling into the wrapper center.
5. Brush the edge of the wrapper with a tiny bit of water, bring the two sides together, and lastly pinch at the top to make a 'half-moon' shape.
6. Holding the top, pleat and pinch the wrappers on each side towards the middle, completely encasing the filling – wet the outside of the wrapper with a little water if needed.
7. Heat a portion of oil in a lidded frying pan using a high temperature setting to fry the bottoms of the gyozas in batches until crispy (2-3 min.).
8. Carefully add water (75 ml) to the pan and cover it with a lid promptly. Wait for the gyozas to steam until the water has evaporated (4-5 min.).
9. The fillings should be thoroughly cooked and the bottoms crispy. Repeat with the remaining gyozas.
10. Serve with your favorite dipping sauce, accompanied with a dot of Nanami paste on top.

Wine Favorites: Enjoy a nicely chilled bottle of NV Champagne or consider a dry English sparkling make a fantastic match with fried dumplings whether they are served hot or cold.

Pepper & Salted Squid

Total Time: 40 min.
Yields Provided: 2 portions

Ingredients Used:

- Sichuan peppercorns (1 tsp.)
- Black peppercorns (1 tsp.)
- Sea salt flakes (1 tbsp.)
- Plain flour (30 g)
- Corn flour (30 g)
- Cleaned squid (400 g)
- Vegetable oil (1 tbsp. + more to fry)
- Spring onions (6 sliced)
- Ginger (thumb-sized)
- Red chilies (3)

Instructions:

1. Slice the chilies. Then, peel and slice the ginger into matchsticks.
2. Toast all the peppercorns in a wok or deep-frying pan using a high temperature setting (30 sec.).
3. Empty them into a container to smash with salt using a mortar and pestle (30 sec.).
4. Combine both types of flour in a bowl, then mix in the peppercorn mixture.
5. Slice the squid tubes (down one side to open out like a book). Lightly score the insides using a crisscross pattern – avoid slicing all the way though.
6. Lastly slice them into edible chunks while slicing the tentacles into similar pieces as well.
7. Heat oil (5-cm deep) in a wok or heavy-based pan until a cube of bread browns in 30 seconds (until it hits 356° Fahrenheit/180° Celsius on a thermometer).
8. Toss the squid in the flour mixture to cover while gently shaking to expel the excess. Use caution and carefully lower into the hot oil - batching will make it easier. Fry until crispy and golden (2-3 min.). Then drain on a bunch of disposable paper towels.
9. Once the squid is prepared, serve as is with a side of lemon wedges or heat oil (1 tbsp.) in a wok over a high heat - stir-fry the ginger, spring onions, and chilies until lightly golden (30 sec.).
10. Fold and toss in all the squid into your serving bowl with a portion of salt as desired.

Wine Favorites: Sauvignon Blanc and Gewurztraminer are dependable options, as are Riesling and Viognier.

Polish Pierogi

Total Time: 1 hr. 10 min.
Yields Provided: 4 portions

Ingredients Used:

The Filling:
- Butter (3 tbsp.)
- Onions (2)
- Grated cheese of your Choice: Smoked twaróg; mild-medium Cheddar or a mixture of Comté & Brilliat-Savarin (180 g)
- Floury potato (1 large)

The Dough:
- Plain flour (300g + more for dusting)
- Egg (2 yolks)
- Melted butter (2 tbsp.)
- Warm water from a pre-boiled kettle (100-120 ml)

Topping & Serving:
- Onion (1)
- Butter - melted (2 tbsp.)
- To Serve: Sour cream

Instructions:

1. First, finely chop the potato and onions.
2. Prepare the filling and the topping by warming three tablespoons of butter in a skillet.
3. Toss in all three onions till caramelized - occasionally stirring. Leave one-third of the onions in the pan to be used for the topping and add the rest (2/3) to a mixing container for now.
4. Use a large bowl to prepare the dough - mixing it by hand to make a ball. Knead the dough on a lightly floured workspace (6-7 min.).
5. Now, use a damp-clean cloth to cover the dough to rest at room temperature (20-30 min.).
6. If using smoked twaróg or another soft cheese, mash it in a bowl with a fork, then transfer it to the bowl with the onions. *Otherwise*, if using a harder grated cheese, toss it into the bowl with the onions.
7. Now, mix in the cooked, diced potato. Taste and season with pepper and salt to your liking.
8. Thinly roll the dough (0.5mm is perfect) on a floured surface to shape the flattened dough. Using a teaspoon, fill the pierogi, then seal. Place it onto a lightly floured surface.
9. Prepare the pierogi in batches using boiling-salted water.
10. Once they float to the top, wait one more minute before removing them using a slotted spoon. Shake off any excess water and transfer to a warm bowl with the two tablespoons melted butter.
11. Before serving, transfer the pierogi to a frying pan and sauté in the butter until golden and crispy (2 min. per side).

12. Serve with the reserved caramelized onions scattered over the top with a side dish of sour cream.

Wine Favorites: Pair your deliciously prepared pierogies with Pinot Noir, a fruit-forward light red wine with a hint of earthiness. You could also go for a medium-bodied aromatic white wine, such as Viognier.

Prawns Pil-Pil

Total Time: 10 min.
Yields Provided: 2 portions

Ingredients Used:

- Olive oil (4 tbsp.)
- Peeled raw king prawns (180 g pkg.)
- Garlic cloves (4)
- Paprika – sweet smoked (2 tsp.)
- Dried chili flakes (1 tsp.)
- Flat-leaf parsley (1 handful/as desired)

    To Serve:
- Crusty bread
- Lemon (half of 1)
- Also Suggested: Non-stick frying pan

Instructions:

1. First remove the peel from the prawns and thinly slice the garlic and parsley. Slice the lemon into wedges to serve.
2. Warm the oil using a medium temperature setting.
3. Toss in the prawns with the garlic to sauté till the prawns have turned pink (3 min.).
4. Mix in the chili flakes, paprika, and a generous pinch of salt to simmer (1 min.). Remove from the burner and garnish with the parsley.
5. Serve with lemon wedges and crusty bread for 'slopping-up' the oil.

Wine Favorites: Enjoy the delicious prawn dish with Sparkling, Sauvignon Blanc, Semillon, Semillon and Sauvignon Blanc, and Riesling.

Salmon Tartare with Lemon & Capers

Total Time: 30 min.
Yields Provided: 6 portions

Ingredients Used:

- Shallot (1)
- Lemon (2)
- Skinless salmon fillet (400 g)
- Smoked salmon (200 g)
- Dill (Chopped to make 2 tbsp.)
- Non-pareille capers (2 tbsp.)
- Crème fraiche (1 tbsp.)
- Lemon/olive oil
- Dijon mustard (1 tbsp.)
- For Serving: Melba toast

Instructions:

1. Rinse and drain the capers. Finely dice the shallot. Juice (1) and slice the lemon into wedges (1).
2. Toss the shallot in the lemon juice to marinate.
3. Slice the salmon into tiny cubes - tossing them into a mixing bowl. Mix in the mustard, capers, dill, crème fraiche, one tablespoon of lemon or olive oil, shallot, and juice.
4. Fold it all together with a portion of salt and pepper to your liking.
5. Serve in neat rounds with melba toast and lemon wedges on the side, and drizzle with a little more lemon oil.

Wine Favorites: Salmon are most often enjoyed with full-bodied white wines like oak-aged Chardonnay, Viognier, White Rioja, Marsanne, White Burgundy, and White Pinot Noir.

Sea Bream Ceviche with Charred Sweetcorn

Total Time: 30 min.
Yields Provided: 2 portions

Ingredients Used:

- Corn-on-the-cob (1)
- Olive oil (as needed)
- Fresh sea bream fillets - skin removed (4)
- Spring onions (2)
- Red chili (1)
- Avocado (half of 1)
- Coriander (1 bunch)

  The Dressing:
- Limes (3)
- Ginger (1 thumb-sized piece)
- Garlic (half of 1 small clove)
- Dried red chili flakes (1 tsp.)

Instructions:

1. Finely chop/slice the onions, chili, and coriander. Peel the avocado, remove the stone, and chop it also. Prepare for the dressing by zesting and juicing the limes. Wash and grate the ginger; then, crush the garlic.
2. Heat the grill using a high temperature setting.
3. Meanwhile, brush the sweetcorn with one tablespoon of olive oil and season well.
4. Put on a baking tray and grill (10-15 min.), turning regularly until the corn is well charred.
5. Remove the kernels by standing the cob on its end and carefully cutting down each side.
6. Slice the sea bream into strips (2-cm) and toss them into a bowl.
7. Whisk all the dressing ingredients with three tablespoons of olive oil and some seasoning – dump it over the fish.
8. Leave to marinate (2 min.).
9. Arrange the fish on a platter, scatter over the charred sweetcorn, spring onions, red chili, and avocado.
10. Spoon over the dressing and scatter with coriander.

Wine Favorites: Pinot grigio, Riesling and Verdelho have a sweetness that marries well with a milder ceviche. Sweet wines are traditionally paired with ceviche. Argentinian chardonnay is another ceviche 'go-to' because the grapes are grown at high elevations and make more acidic wines.

Spicy Prawn Cocktail

Total Time: 15 min.
Yields Provided: 6 portions

Ingredients Used:

- Egg (1 yolk)
- White wine vinegar (1 tbsp.)
- English mustard (.5 tbsp.)
- Vegetable oil (250 ml)
- Tomato ketchup (3 tbsp.)
- Worcestershire sauce (.5 tsp.)
- Brandy (1 tsp.)
- Salt & cayenne pepper
- Lemon juice
- Baby gem lettuce (2 - shredded)
- Cooked peeled prawns (75 g)

  For Serving:
- Buttered brown bread
- Lemon wedges

Instructions:

1. Whisk the egg yolk with the wine vinegar and mustard in a big mixing container using electric beaters.
2. Slowly drizzle in the vegetable oil, whisking all the time, until all the oil is used up and you have a mayonnaise. (250ml store-bought mayo - attempt to purchase one with organic eggs for the best flavor).
3. Stir into the mayo, ketchup, brandy, and Worcestershire sauce.
4. Mix in some cayenne pepper, salt, and lemon juice t (additional ketchup for a sweeter sauce).
   Shred the lettuce and arrange in serving glasses.
5. Load them by piling the cooked-peeled prawns into each glass and spooning it as desired with cocktail sauce. Serve with lemon wedges and buttered brown bread.

Wine Favorites: Shrimp Cocktail is deliciously served with white wines such as Riesling, Muscadet, Torrontés, Prosecco, Pinot Blanc, and Sauvignon Blanc.

Chapter 7: Other Italian Favorites

Burrata al Tartufo

Total Time: 15 min.
Yields Provided: 4 portions

Ingredients Used:

- Burrata (2)
- *To Drizzle*: Olive oil
- *Optional Garnish*: Truffle
- *To Serve*: Crispbreads

- *The Sauce*:
- Mushrooms (100 g)
- Sunflower oil (25 ml + 1 tsp.)
- Truffles (10 g - minced)

Instructions:

1. Prepare the truffle sauce by blitzing the mushrooms in a mini food processor till they are in fine pieces.
2. Set up a skillet using a medium temperature setting to warm oil (1 tsp.).
3. When heated, sauté the mushrooms till done and reduced (3-4 min.). Let them cool and combine with the remainder of the sauce components.
4. Place the container in the refrigerator to infuse for several hours (even better if overnight).
5. Now, add the truffle sauce to a big piping bag fitted with a small nozzle or snip a hole in a plastic bag.
6. Pierce the base of each burrata and use the piping bag to fill with the sauce until each one is extra plump - not overstuffed.
7. Serve them with drizzles of oil, shavings of truffle, freshly cracked black pepper, and salt. Serve with crispy bread.

Wine Favorites: Since the dish will be served with olive oil, a powerful Grüner Veltliner is the finest match, although a traditional Grüner Veltliner would also pair too.

Burrata Bruschetta

Total Time: 45 min.
Yields Provided: 2 portions

Ingredients Used:

- Coppa - capocollo/Italian style cured pork shoulder (100 g)
- Burrata/mozzarella (250 g ball)
- Figs (2)
- Runny honey (a drizzle)
- Thyme (2 sprigs)
- Toasted ciabatta - sliced
- Hazelnuts (20 g)
- Basil (1 small bunch)

  To Drizzle:
- Olive oil (as needed)
- Onions - pickled (20 g)
- Vinegar - balsamic used (to taste)

  The Jam:
- Red onions (500 g)
- Olive oil (2 tbsp.)
- Caster sugar (85 g)
- Vinegar – red wine type used (50 ml)
- Port (50 ml)

Instructions:

1. Toast and chop the nuts and tear the basil apart. Thinly slice the pork and onions, then - slice the ciabatta into 1.5 cm slices.
2. Prepare the onions in the oil with a pinch of salt for ten minutes with a lid on the pan till they start to soften.
3. Mix in the sugar and continue to simmer - top on - till they are softened.
4. Mix in and gently simmer the port and vinegar till the onions have a jam-like consistency (10 min.).
5. Wait for the jam mixture to cool, keeping any leftovers in the refrigerator in a sterilized jar.
6. An hour before serving, remove the pork/coppa and burrata from the refrigerator to come to room temperature.
7. Preheat the oven to reach Heat the oven to 392° Fahrenheit/200° Celsius. Break apart the burrata.
8. Slice the figs - lengthways – with a drizzle with honey. Garnish them to your liking with a pinch of salt, pepper, and thyme.
9. Add the mixture to a baking tray and warm.
10. Spread the ciabatta with a portion of the onion jam, top with the burrata, basil, hazelnuts, pepper to taste, and a spritz of olive oil.
11. Serve the mix and juices over the heated figs. Serve them on a tray with the coppa and pickled onions to the side, and a spritz of vinegar.

Wine Favorites: A red wine such as Pinot Noir is a perfect match.

Chicory with Grains & Mixed Pulses

Total Time: 45 min.
Yields Provided: 4 portions

Ingredients Used:

- Borlotti/Cranberry beans (400 g tin)
- Cherry tomatoes (1 handful)
- Light olive oil (100 ml + extra for frying)
- White wine vinegar (250 ml)
- Caster sugar (250 g)
- Red onions (2 sliced into 1-cm rings)
- Anchovy fillets in olive oil (4)
- Panko breadcrumbs (50 g)
- Chicory (2 heads - halved)
- Cooked puy lentils (100 g)
- Cooked spelt (100 g)
- Cooked risina or cannellini beans (50 g)
- Lemon (half of 1 - juiced)

Instructions:

1. Prepare and simmer the borlotti beans and juices in a pan with the tomatoes. Blitz in a blender/food processor, adding the olive oil (machine in operation). Once it is velvety smooth, season to your liking and put aside to cool.
2. Toss the sugar with the vinegar in a pan with the onion rings. Sauté them until softened (10 min.). Scoop them out using a slotted spoon – set aside for now.
3. Warm a tablespoon of oil and prepare the anchovy fillets while using the back of a wooden spoon to break them down. Now mix in the breadcrumbs, stirring until they are golden brown. Scoop into a piece of kitchen parchment paper.
4. Warm a griddle pan and brush the flat side of each half of chicory with oil. Char-grill until marked (2 to 3 min.).
5. Using the back of a metal spoon, smooth a circle of borlotti purée onto two plates, then divide over the onions and the lentils, spelt and beans.
6. Add the chicory, lemon juice, additional oil, and salt.
7. Garnish with breadcrumbs as desired.

Wine Favorites: Chianti, Cabernet Franc, Beaujolais Villages, or Syrah are excellent options. For white wine, try a Chardonnay or Vouvray

Grilled Peaches with Burrata

Total Time: 20 min.
Yields Provided: 2-3 portions

Ingredients Used:

- Peaches - ripe but firm (2)
- Olive oil
- Rocket/arugula (2 handfuls)
- Serrano ham (6 slices)
- Burrata (1 ball)
- Basil (1 small bunch)
- Toasted pine nuts (2 tbsp.)

- *Optional for Serving*: Crusty bread

  The Dressing:
- White balsamic vinegar (2 tbsp.)
- Olive oil (3 tbsp.)
- Runny honey (1 tsp.)
- Red chili (1)
- Garlic (half of 1 clove)

Instructions:

1. Load a mixing container to prepare the dressing by whisking the olive oil with the vinegar and honey. Then, finely mince and toss in the chili and garlic.
2. Use a high temperature setting to warm a griddle pan.
3. Slice the peaches into halves and trash the stones. Then, brush them with oil and griddle all till caramelized and charred.
4. Scatter the rocket on a platter. Drape over - the ham, add the peaches, and arrange the burrata in the middle.
5. Discard the garlic clove mix from the dressing, then spoon over everything. Scatter over the basil and pine nuts.
6. Serve with crusty bread for a special treat.

Wine Favorites: Pair It - Albariño, Muscat, Riesling, Viognier, warm-climate Chardonnay, and South African Chenin Blanc are suggested options with the peaches.

Grilled Veggie Antipasti

Total Time: 30 min. (+) marinating time
Yields Provided: 4-6 portions

Ingredients Used:

- Red - green & yellow peppers (1 each)
- Medium zucchinis/courgettes (3)
- Medium eggplant/aubergines (2)
- Whole cloves (3)
- Thyme sprigs (as desired)
- Olive oil
- Sherry vinegar

Instructions:

1. Remove the seeds and slice the peppers into quarters. Slice the aubergines and courgettes into one-cm slices. Smash the garlic cloves.
2. Toss the peppers in a mixing bowl with two tablespoons of olive oil and seasoning to your liking with three bowls ready to prepare.
3. Heat a big griddle pan (med-high temperature setting). Griddle the pepper slices in batches till they are softened, and grill marked.
4. When ready add them into one of the bowls and cover so the residual heat and steam will further soften the peppers.
5. Repeat this process with the zucchini and eggplant, making sure *all* the veggies are tender before tipping them into the additional two serving dishes.
6. Once all the vegetables are cooked, add garlic, thyme, and a splash of vinegar with another two tablespoons of oil to each bowl.
7. Leave at room temperature for a minimum of one hour to marinate if you are eating that day. *Otherwise*, chill for up to three days in the fridge.
8. Serve at room temperature.

Wine Favorites: Choose reds with decent acidity. Try Barbera, Montepulciano, Chianti, Brunello di Montalcino, and Valpolicella.

Italian Scotch Olives

Total Time: 35 min.
Yields Provided: 6 portions

Ingredients Used:

- Olive oil (1 tbsp.)
- Onion (1 small)
- Fennel seeds (1 tsp.)
- Garlic (1 clove)
- Sage & thyme (.5 tsp. each)
- Red wine (100 ml)
- Sausage meat (300 g)
- Gordal* olives in brine
- Plain flour, seasoned (150 g)
- Egg yolks (6) whisked with milk (3 tbsp.)
- Panko breadcrumbs (200 g)
- To Deep Fry: Vegetable oil
- Optional to Serve: Mayonnaise

Instructions:

1. Do the prep. Finely chop the garlic and onion. Mince the thyme and sage. Dab the olives dry and discard the pits.
2. Warm olive oil in a skillet and sauté the onion (5 min.).
3. Then, toss in the fennel and garlic to sauté (3 min.).
4. Mix in the wine and herbs – reducing it to a glaze.
5. Spread the mixture over a platter to cool for several minutes.
6. Mix the onion mix and sausage in a mixing bowl with a pinch of pepper and salt. Then portion it into balls (about the size of a quail's egg).
7. Wrap the meat around the olives till they are covered fully.
8. Roll the scotch olives in the seasoned flour platter to thoroughly cover.
9. Dip the scotch olives individually in the egg yolk, let the excess drip off, then coat thoroughly in the breadcrumbs - ready for cooking.
10. Fill a pan with oil (not over 1/3-full) and warm it until a cube of bread browns in 25 seconds (374° Fahrenheit/190° Celsius).
11. Fry the scotch olives in batches until deeply golden and crisp, and the meat is cooked through (3-4 min.). Scoop them out to drain on kitchen paper before serving.

*Note: Due to its rounded appearance and substantial bulk, the name "gordal" means "the fat one" (over 6 g). It has a strong, meaty texture and a subtle, delicate flavor reminiscent to manzanilla.

Wine Favorites: Pair green olives with Cabernet Franc.

Marinated Melon & Bocconcini

Total Time: 15 min. (+) marinating time
Yields Provided: portions

Ingredients Used:

- *Galia melon (half of 1)
- Charentais or cantaloupe melon (half of 1)
- Buffalo mozzarella bocconcini (250 g tub)
- Oregano - leaves picked (Several sprigs)

  The Dressing:
- Olive oil (2 tbsp.)
- Vinegar - white balsamic type suggested (2 tbsp.)
- Red chili (1)

Instructions:

1. Use a melon baller or teaspoon to scoop out balls of melon and put in a serving dish.
2. Whisk the balsamic and oil together. Finely chop and mix in the chili and seasoning as desired.
3. Drain and add the bocconcini to the melon balls and splash with the dressing. Wait about ½ hour before scattering the leaves of oregano leaves over the top - just before serving.
4. *Note*: Created in the 1970s, galia is a cross between cantaloupe and honeydew melon.

Wine Favorites: Enjoy this dish with Californian Chardonnay or Chilean Sauvignon Blanc.

Potato Dumplings with Cabbage & Cheese

Total Time: 30 min.
Yields Provided: 4 portions

Ingredients Used:

- Giovanni Rana's readymade potato dumplings (500 g)
- Mild - Provolizie Auricchio/provolone (16 oz. pkg./as desired)
- Cabbage (1 heart)
- White onion (half of 1) or shallot (1)
- Butter (50 g butter
- Organic walnuts - shelled (40 g)
- Vegetable stock
- Sage leaves (10)
- Saffron (1 sachet)
- Salt & Black pepper

Instructions:

1. Prepare a saucepan with oil/butter to sauté the minced onion till it is transparent.
2. Finely chop and add in the cabbage while stirring with a portion of vegetable broth, pepper, and salt. Simmer for about ten minutes.
3. At that time, mix in the saffron using a hand mixer till it is silky.
4. Cook the dumplings in f boiling salted water.
5. Melt the butter with the sage and add in the nuts with a small amount of cooking water from the dumplings.
6. Drain the gnocchi till it is 'al dente' after they have floated to the surface.
7. Drain and sauté them with the buttered sage.
8. Mix in the provolone in with a splash of cooking water and serve with the creamed cabbage.

Wine Favorites: Your wine selection includes Pinot grigio, Sauvignon Blanc, Cabernet Sauvignon, Syrah.

Prickly Lettuce Pizza

Total Time: 60 min.
Yields Provided: 4 portions

Ingredients Used:

- Brisé pastry - in English - sturdy pastry dough (250 g)
- Prickly lettuce (2 heads)
- Black olives (100 g)
- Organic* raisin (50 g)
- Garlic clove (1)
- Organic* pine nuts (50 g)
- Cannamela red hot chili pepper (1 small)
- Olive oil

Instructions:

1. Do the prep before you begin making your delicious pizza.
2. Remove the pits from the olives. Thoroughly rinse the lettuce, chop it, and add it to a saucepan using a high temperature setting to reduce its liquid content. Soak the raisins in water.
3. In another pan, heat oil to sauté the hot pepper and garlic.
4. Once the garlic is browning, add the olives, raisins, pine nuts, and lastly the lettuce. Simmer the mixture for several minutes.
5. Preheat the oven to 392° Fahrenheit/200° Celsius.
6. Cover a baking tray with a layer of parchment baking paper, spread out the pastry on it, and cover it with the prepared mixture - taking care to discard the garlic.
7. Bake for approximately 35 minutes and cool before serving.
8. * Noberasco for example is a great organic choice.

Wine Favorites: Have some fun with one of these delightful options.

- Masseria Altemura Rosato Salento IGT
- Santa Margherita Pinot Grigio Valdadige
- Tenuta Cà Bolani Pinot Grigio Friuli Aquileia DOC Superiore
- Tenuta Cà Bolani Müller Thurgau Frizzante delle Venezie IGT

Ricotta Gnudi with Sage Butter

Total Time: 30 min. active (+) 2 days to drain & chill
Yields Provided: 4 portions

Ingredients Used:

- Ricotta (500 g)
- Grated parmesan (75 g)
- White pepper & fresh nutmeg (as desired)
- Semolina (500 g)
- Butter (150 g)
- Sage (1 bunch)

Instructions:

1. Scoop the ricotta into a sieve over a mixing container and cover. Pop it in the refrigerator to drain (overnight is suggested).
2. When ready to prepare the following day, add the ricotta to a fresh bowl with the nutmeg, seasoning, and parmesan - thoroughly combine.
3. Pour half the semolina onto a small tray. Scoop large teaspoons of the ricotta mix and roll into little dumpling shapes.
4. Now, gently roll them in the semolina until coated. Then add the remainder of the semolina to thoroughly cover the balls - chill them overnight.
5. When you are almost ready to serve the gnudi, warm the butter in a big skillet till the mixture is foaming.
6. At that time, fold in the sage leaves and continue cooking until crispy and scoop them onto kitchen paper.
7. Take the butter off the heat once the gnudi (gnocchi-like dumplings made with ricotta cheese) are ready.
8. Now, warm a large - wide pan with boiling-salted water and prepare the gnudi in batches to help eliminate sticking.
9. Tweak the temperature till the water is gently simmering (3 min.).
10. Once they are floating, use a slotted spoon to scoop them into the butter pan.
11. For the following batch, put the butter pan back on the heat and warm the butter before spooning over the gnudi.
12. Serve in warm bowls with the sage and extra parmesan as desired.

Wine Favorites: Sangiovese wines, such as Chianti Classico or Brunello di Montalcino are an amazing Tuscan match for the Gnudi.

Tomatoes & Lardo on Toast

Total Time: 35 min.
Yields Provided: 4 portions

Ingredients Used:

- Basil (50 g)
- Sunflower oil (150 ml)
- Olive oil (as needed)
- Large ripe tomatoes (4)
- Red wine vinegar (1 tbsp.)
- Sourdough (4 slices)
- Garlic (half of 1 clove)
- Lardo/cured pork fat (12 thin slices)
- Also Needed: Kitchen torch

Instructions:

1. Blanch the basil in a pan of boiling water (10 sec.). Immediately tip them into a container of iced water for five minutes. Then drain and squeeze dry.
2. Toss the basil in a food processor with the oil and a pinch of salt to pulse till it is velvety (5 min.).
3. Cover a colander over a bowl in the kitchen sink with muslin and pour in the sunflower oil.
4. Gather up the edges, tie in a knot and hang over the bowl (1-2 hr.).
5. Thickly slice the tomatoes and combine with oil (1 tbsp.), red wine vinegar, and some seasoning in a mixing bowl. Stir and wait for an hour with it at room temperature.
6. Toast the sourdough slices and rub with the garlic clove.
7. Top with the tomatoes, a generous drizzle of the basil oil, and the lardo slices.
8. Blowtorch the lardo or put under a hot grill to lightly melt.

Wine Favorites: You have several options including Falanghina del Sannio Taburno 2018 Fontanavecchia, Vermentino di Gallura Sup, Maìa 2016 Siddùra, or Colli Orientali del Friuli Ribolla Gialla 2017 Torre Rosazza.

Italian Favorite Bread Options

Combo Flatbread with Walnuts, Pears & Gorgonzola

Total Time: 45 min.
Yields Provided: 8-10 portions

Ingredients Used:

- Red-skinned pears (2)
- Walnuts (15)
- Gorgonzola dolce (diced weight @ 150g)

  Optional for Serving: Fig jam or chutney

  The Bread:
- Olive oil
- Strong bread flour/extra-fine & unbleached (300 g + more for dusting)
- Sea salt flakes (1 tsp.)
- Caster sugar (1 tsp.)
- Sachet fast-action dried yeast (7 g)
- Natural yogurt (1 tbsp.)

Instructions:

1. Remove the core and thinly slice the pears into wedges. Roughly break the nuts. Then, discard the rind from the gorgonzola dolce and dice.
2. Now, whisk/mix the flour with sugar, salt, and yeast in a big mixing container.
3. Use another container to combine the yogurt with olive oil (1 tbsp.) and warm water (175 ml). Now, slowly mix into the flour to form a soft dough.
4. Tip onto a lightly floured work surface and knead until smooth and springy (8-10 min.). Use minimal flour and place the dough in a bowl, cover, and wait one hour for it to rise/doubled in its size.
5. Heat the oven to reach 392° Fahrenheit/200° Celsius.
6. Scoop the dough onto a work surface while pressing it into a large rectangle (25-cm x 35-cm), then put on a large baking sheet.
7. Lightly brush its surface with olive oil. Then push in the pears and walnut halves all over.
8. Dot with the gorgonzola and bake until puffed and golden (15-20 min.). Drizzle with a tiny bit of oil, then serve with fig jam or chutney as desired.

Wine Favorites: Chardonnay is a classic white varietal is one of the top pairings for many bold cheese types due to its incredibly versatile nature. Oaked Chardonnay elevates the sweet notes of Gorgonzola dolce, while unoaked Chardonnay contrasts the pungent aromas of mountain Gorgonzola.

Focaccia

Total Time: 45 min. (+) proof time
Yields Provided: 6 portions

Ingredients Used:

- Olive oil (9 tbsp.)
- Rosemary leaves - picked (3 sprigs)
- Strong white bread flour (300 g)
- Sachet fast-action yeast (7 g)
- Sea salt flakes (1 tsp. + extra for sprinkling)

Instructions:

1. Pour oil (6 tbsp.) in a bowl with the rosemary and let it rest while you make the bread.
2. Whisk the flour with the yeast and the remaining three tablespoons of olive oil in a bowl with one teaspoon of sea salt flakes. Gradually add water (175 ml) and mix until you have a sticky dough.
3. Knead the dough on a lightly oiled work surface (6-8 min.). Scoop it into a fresh, lightly oiled container, cover with a kitchen towel, and let it rise till it is about doubled in size (1 hr.).
4. Oil a heavy baking tray, 'punch down' the dough - then knead briefly.
5. Scoop the dough onto the baking sheet and form into a 20-cm x 28-cm rectangle. Wait for it to rise again (½ hour).
6. Set the oven temperature to reach 392° Fahrenheit/200° Celsius.
7. Make a few "dimples" in the dough top with your fingertips. Then sprinkle it using the rosemary-infused oil and leaves with a sprinkle of sea salt flakes.
8. Bake it until golden brown (20 min.).
9. Cover loosely with foil to create a bit of steam to keep the crust soft. Wait for it to cool.
10. Drizzle with a little more oil before serving as desired.

Wine Favorites: Focaccia pair best with white wines such as Sauvignon Blanc, Gavi, Chardonnay, and Champagne. Light red wines such as Beaujolais can also be served.

Grilled Fish Recipes:

1. **Grilled Lemon Herb Sea Bass:**

   - Ingredients:

     - 2 sea bass fillets
     - 1 lemon (juiced)
     - 2 tbsp olive oil
     - 2 cloves garlic (minced)
     - Fresh herbs (rosemary, thyme)
     - Salt and pepper to taste

   - Instructions:

     - Preheat the grill to medium-high heat.
     - In a bowl, mix lemon juice, olive oil, minced garlic, salt, and pepper.
     - Brush the fish fillets with the marinade.
     - Grill the fillets for 4-5 minutes per side, until fish flakes easily.
     - Garnish with fresh herbs before serving.

2. **Mediterranean Grilled Branzino:**

   - Ingredients:

     - 2 branzino, gutted and scaled
     - 2 tbsp olive oil
     - 1 tsp dried oregano
     - 1 tsp paprika
     - Salt and pepper to taste
     - Lemon wedges for serving

   - Instructions:

     - Preheat the grill to medium-high heat.
     - Rub fish with olive oil, oregano, paprika, salt, and pepper.
     - Grill for 6-8 minutes per side until the skin is crispy and the flesh is cooked.
     - Serve with lemon wedges.

3. **Tuscan Grilled Swordfish:**

   - Ingredients:

     - 2 swordfish steaks
     - 3 tbsp balsamic vinegar
     - 2 tbsp olive oil

- 1 tsp dried rosemary
- Salt and pepper to taste
  - Instructions:
    - Preheat the grill to medium heat.
    - Mix balsamic vinegar, olive oil, rosemary, salt, and pepper.
    - Marinate swordfish in the mixture for 30 minutes.
    - Grill for 5-7 minutes per side until grill marks appear.

4. **Grilled Salmon with Dijon Glaze:**

  - Ingredients:
    - 2 salmon fillets
    - 2 tbsp Dijon mustard
    - 2 tbsp honey
    - 1 tbsp soy sauce
    - 1 tsp minced garlic
    - Salt and pepper to taste
  - Instructions:
    - Preheat the grill to medium-high heat.
    - Mix Dijon mustard, honey, soy sauce, garlic, salt, and pepper.
    - Brush the salmon with the glaze and grill for 4-5 minutes per side.

5. **Lemon Garlic Grilled Shrimp:**

  - Ingredients:
    - 1 lb large shrimp, peeled and deveined
    - 3 tbsp olive oil
    - Zest and juice of 1 lemon
    - 2 cloves garlic (minced)
    - Fresh parsley (chopped)
    - Salt and pepper to taste
  - Instructions:
    - Preheat the grill to medium heat.
    - Toss shrimp with olive oil, lemon zest, lemon juice, minced garlic, salt, and pepper.
    - Grill for 2-3 minutes per side until opaque.
    - Sprinkle with fresh parsley before serving.

Fried Fish Recipes:

1. **Classic Italian Fried Fish:**

- Ingredients:

  - 2 white fish fillets (cod or haddock)
  - 1 cup all-purpose flour
  - 2 eggs (beaten)
  - Salt and pepper to taste
  - Vegetable oil for frying

- Instructions:

  - Heat oil in a pan over medium heat.
  - Dredge fish in flour, dip in beaten eggs, and fry for 3-4 minutes per side until golden brown.

2. **Crispy Lemon Parmesan Fried Tilapia:**

- Ingredients:

  - 2 tilapia fillets
  - 1 cup breadcrumbs
  - 1/2 cup grated Parmesan
  - Zest of 1 lemon
  - Salt and pepper to taste
  - Vegetable oil for frying

- Instructions:

  - Combine breadcrumbs, Parmesan, lemon zest, salt, and pepper.
  - Coat tilapia in the mixture and fry for 3-4 minutes per side until crispy.

3. **Fried Calamari Rings:**

- Ingredients:

  - 1/2 lb calamari rings
  - 1 cup buttermilk
  - 1 cup flour
  - 1 tsp paprika
  - Salt and pepper to taste
  - Vegetable oil for frying

- Instructions:

  - Soak calamari in buttermilk for 30 minutes.
  - Combine flour, paprika, salt, and pepper.
  - Dredge calamari in the flour mixture and fry for 2-3 minutes until golden.

4. **Lemon Garlic Butter Fried Red Snapper:**

- Ingredients:

- 2 red snapper fillets
- 1/2 cup flour
- 2 tbsp butter
- 2 cloves garlic (minced)
- Zest and juice of 1 lemon
- Salt and pepper to taste

- Instructions:

  - Dredge snapper in flour and fry in butter for 4-5 minutes per side.
  - Add minced garlic, lemon zest, and lemon juice in the last minute of cooking.

5. **Italian Style Fried Anchovies:**

- Ingredients:

  - 1/2 lb fresh anchovies, cleaned
  - 1 cup semolina flour
  - 1 tsp dried oregano
  - Salt and pepper to taste
  - Vegetable oil for frying

- Instructions:

  - Coat anchovies in semolina flour mixed with oregano, salt, and pepper.
  - Fry for 2-3 minutes until crispy.
  - Serve immediately.

Conclusion

I hope you have enjoyed each delicious Italian first course meal in your new copy of *Italian cookbook*. Each recipe was prepared for you to enjoy meals in the same manner as everyone in Italy. The next step is to simply decide which one to try first.

You have tons of varieties to choose from with just the first batch of delicious appetizers enclosed in your new cookbook.

I know you are ready and excited to begin your new way of dining (just like the pros)! You set the scene using delicious Italian cuisine.

Lastly, if you found your new cookbook useful in any way with its array of wine suggestions, a review on Amazon is always appreciated!

Made in the USA
Las Vegas, NV
18 December 2023

83103552R00046